FACILITATION

MADE EASY

FACILITATION MADE EASY - A Survivor's Guide to Great Meetings

Cover Design by: Flip Design Studio, Inc.
Interior Design by: Heather Kilcrease

ISBN 978-0-9976076-1-1

Published by: Write Way Publishing Company, LLC

FACILITATION MADE EASY

A Survivor's Guide to Great Meetings

CONTENTS

WHAT PEOPLE ARE SAYING

"Not being in the public affairs sector of my business, *Facilitation Made Easy* gave me a boost of confidence and was especially useful helping me prepare for public hearings on a major federal government project. In addition, I was able to keep over 30 Type-A personalities engaged and focused on our objectives for the better part of a week. A number of people, including a professional trainer with 35+ years of experience, cited specific techniques they liked and planned to use in the future.

I recommend this book to anyone and everyone who participates in, or has attempted to moderate, meetings of any type, as the information is well-organized and packaged in a way that makes it very easy to apply. It ... breaks down the challenging elements of day-to-day business and provides techniques to improve the process."

— Mike Glenn, Program Manager, Department of Energy,
National Nuclear Security Administration

"*Facilitation Made Easy* has been a real gift to me by providing numerous tips for improving my facilitating skills. As important as it is to know what to do; knowing what NOT to do is equally necessary.

Each easy read section is full of little nuggets of advice that are sometimes small but critical to a successful workshop or retreat. I find myself referring to this book prior to my events."

— JoAnne Muegge, Certified Coach/Facilitator

"As an experienced meeting facilitator, I'm frequently looking for "best in class" practices to serve my clients well. Mary Tomlinson's book, *Facilitation Made Easy*, delivers from beginning to end. I've had the privilege of participating in meetings facilitated by Mary and can attest that the book is written from the perspective of an excellent practitioner on the art of facilitating."

— Sharon Epps, President, Kinetic Consulting, LLC

"*Facilitation Made Easy* is a must read for anyone wanting to host a successful meeting. Mary gives a practical, applicable and easy to implement guide to facilitation. And it is all served up in a personable, engaging and fun to read style that is quintessential 'Mary.'"

— Jody J. Dreyer, Author and Business Advisor

INTRODUCTION

Meetings—most of us hate them, and yet our schedules are often full of them.

When I was at Disney, meetings were the daily currency of how to do business, and any typical day had eight to nine meetings back to back. I have vivid memories of these days, usually without time to eat (unless you count scarfing down a stale donut) or even to dash to the restroom. And then came the concept of "standing meetings" (an ongoing, repeatable meeting on your calendar, weekly, or monthly) which had the capacity to tie-up one's schedule for years. When I was leaving Disney, I looked at what was scheduled on my calendar one year into the future and noted that it was already booked full of standing meetings. That was a depressing moment.

And, if thinking about all our regular meetings wasn't bad enough, the thought of a full-day retreat could give us hives. We would now be in the same room with the same people for eight (or more) hours. It's no surprise that many of those retreats were painfully long and unproductive.

Sometimes we would bring in an outside facilitator who brought new hope, fresh air, and new energy and created a different dynamic with the team, the exercises, and the outcomes. I was always intrigued at how much a good facilitator could change a meeting's dynamic.

After eighteen years at Disney attending thousands of meetings and the last fourteen years in my own business, facilitating planning retreats and meetings for five to two hundred people, I'm thrilled to share my lessons learned so that my bruises and success stories can serve others well.

The genesis of this book came after one challenging facilitated retreat when a very satisfied client asked me to come back to teach their HR professional how to run effective meetings. I began to make my notes and started to realize just how much there was to share—both what to do and NOT to do—and this book began to emerge.

Over the years, I've also spoken with many of my facilitator friends who have allowed me to share their tricks of the trade as well.

My hope is that you embrace the challenge of facilitation, and in our journey together over the next pages, you take away some new insights and get a chuckle or two along the way at my expense.

CHAPTER 1
So You've Been Asked to Facilitate a Meeting

Think of the best meeting or planning retreat you have ever attended.

—What made it great?

I would guess it was a well-organized, on-time, on-topic, engaging, energizing, and productive meeting.

Are you thinking, *I've never had one of those?*

—Ouch! Read on.

Try this one (which unfortunately may be easier).

Think of the worst meeting or planning retreat you have ever attended.

—What made it miserable?

I would guess it was the opposite of the meeting described earlier. It probably started late, ended late, was unorganized and full of rabbit trails, had long tedious presentations, included some individuals who monopolized the discussion, and had too much time sitting and listening, all of which created a lack of clarity and accomplishment. Does this sound more familiar?

The history and root of the word "facilitate" is from a French word "faciliter," first mentioned in 1610, which meant "to render easy."

As a facilitator, your clients want your help in "making it easy" to:
- Meet their objectives for the session.
- Find ways to make it interesting.
- Stay on topic.
- Keep to a schedule.
- Ensure that everyone is engaged.
- Provide an outside, objective, and experienced viewpoint.
- And, most importantly, make *them* look good!

There are, in fact, true joys of facilitating meetings that we explore in this book—**but quite often, our joys of facilitating are buried underneath the challenges of:**

- **Unrealistic expectations from the client/leader who says:**
  "We need to build a stronger team, create our annual plan, and develop a new compensation model in two hours—can we do that?"

- **Unexpected logistical changes—such as the room set-up:**
  "Yes, I know we said we would arrange four small tables in a room with windows for your group; but we had to move some rooms around and thought this small executive conference room with no windows and one table could work for your two-day retreat."

Despite the challenges, the joys of facilitating can be unbelievably rewarding, and even exhilarating, when you can:

- *Walk confidently into a retreat room* with people you have never met, knowing that you are prepared, knowledgeable about the team and their issues, and ready to embark on an incredible adventure.

- *Transform a group of unwilling and somewhat cynical people* into those who not only have come together to solve a problem but also are laughing and developing as a cohesive team during the process.

- *Create an instantly engaging environment* where teams can solve their own challenges and feel great about the process and outcomes.

- *Enjoy a moment during your facilitating day by stopping and listening* to your room full of energized people in their small groups discussing, laughing, working, and solving problems.

- *See your thoughtful agenda achieve its desired goals* in an interactive and energizing way.

- *Hear comments like*

    "The time went by so fast!" *or* "I really didn't want to come, but I am now so glad I did—this was great!"

But, as a facilitator, part of the joy is knowing that big problems can represent big opportunities to solve.

Some of my favorite experiences have been to facilitate:

- *Agreement around faculty compensation.*

    Prior to hiring me as their facilitator, they shared that in previous meetings, people had gotten so angry that they had walked out of their internal meetings on this understandably emotionally charged topic.

- *A new Community Advisory Council session given the task to create consensus* on how to spend two hundred million dollars.

    A tough job, but somebody had to do it, and it was harder than you might think.

- *A longstanding hospital with an organizational culture that truthfully didn't feel they had any competition,* so the pervasive attitude was "why bother?"

    The initial reaction to our service culture development work was "Look, Lady, I'm here to save their behind, not kiss it."

- *Family communication planning work on vision and values* with high net worth families when emotions (and financial stakes) were high.

- *A business transition plan from father to son for a seventy-five year-old family-owned business. The two family members had very different leadership styles and both of them were in the room.*

- *Organizational work processes among business groups who had tried it before and failed,* so frustrations were high and hope for any positive outcome was low.

It can be done! As the facilitator, you have the opportunity to diagnose, design, and facilitate solutions to "make it easy" for the groups you serve. The trick is to make it look easy for you!

Let's go on a step-by-step journey together as I share my successful and not-so-successful experiences and what has worked consistently with hundreds of meetings and retreats.

I will share clear steps to ensure your success in the process of facilitating a meeting. This book will explore each of the steps and show you how to apply them to your meetings. The strategies in total may seem overwhelming at first, but each step intentionally builds upon the previous for a successful facilitation. In the note section on page 91, jot down ideas best for you.

For easier reading, let's define terms:

Facilitator —

> Someone asked to help create an outcome for a meeting (which could be planning, brainstorming, problem solving, team building, etc.)
>
> All of these elements involve an up-front understanding of the need for the meeting, design of the agenda, facilitation of the day, and summary wrap-up. Facilitators should work with the meeting planner to ensure the set-up is as needed.

Meeting Planner —

> Someone asked to handle all the logistics of the day, including working with the venue to determine the exact location, needed equipment, and the food, beverage, and snack menus for the day.

Retreat/Session —

The actual meeting, which could last an hour to several days. Many companies call it a retreat since it is often away from the office, but many host on-site meetings as well.

Client/Leader —

Your "client" could be your boss, a leader in the organization, or your paid client if you facilitate for a living. Ultimately, this is the person who contacts you and the one you want to make happy when all is said and done.

CHAPTER 2
What to Know Before You Go

As with most things in life, knowing where you are going is key to your success.

As the Cheshire Cat said to Alice in Wonderland (paraphrased),

> "If you don't know where you are going, any road will get you there."

Many times clients will call and say they want a "planning retreat." Realize this is not the destination. To define where you are going, you will need to truly understand your client's hopes, goals, and definitions of success. From there, the plan will unfold.

Lesson Learned in This Process

Some clients have called and said, "I need a half-day retreat—what does that cost?"

I've learned the hard way that I shouldn't respond immediately with a fee—but, instead, should ask some key questions. More than once, without asking questions, I finalized the pricing for a half-day engagement, but then, based on the client's true needs and goals, the scope continued to expand and change.

It turned into a full-day (and beyond) project.

I have only myself to blame. Agreeing to a time frame and pricing ahead of understanding what needs to be done can result in a frustrating experience for the facilitator.

I encourage you to ask for a budget but not to be discouraged if you do not get a straight answer. I have rarely found clients who will share the budget up front. It also may be helpful to ask

- If other meetings related to the topic will be held in advance of the session.
- Who the key leaders in the room will be.
- If there are other issues that will need to be addressed. (By asking this, I recently discovered a major email controversy in an organization that affected everyone in the room—good to know!)

PRE-EVENT SURVEYS

To ensure that you are getting to the right place in the right way, you first have to start with client questions (and remember your client may be your boss, another leader, or the person who has hired your contracted services).

Ask questions such as:

- What is the goal of the session?
- What is the background that has gotten you to this point?
- What will success look like in terms of what people will do differently as a result of this session?
- Tell me about the group dynamics:
    - Do participants know each other?
    - Do they like each other?
    - Have they worked together before?
    - Are they dependent on one another or independent?

Most leaders can tell you what they see as success for the retrea ̩ut just don't know how to get there—thus the reason they need you!

After your questions have been answered and you have finalized the contract, you are on your way.

Congratulations!

Next, as you begin to craft a draft agenda, consider pre-event surveys, as they are a fabulous means of connecting with your participants.

Participants surveyed will give you as the facilitator keen insights into what you are walking into, their expectations, and their areas of need.

GIVING PEOPLE "**VOICE**" IS A KEY TO SUCCESS IN FACILITATION.

It doesn't have to be a complicated process.

I use Survey Monkey (*SurveyMonkey.com*) for larger groups of fifteen or more and one-on-one phone interviews if the group is small.

Participant answers always reveal the real issues in the group and may suggest needed keys to the agenda design.

If you want them to be honest with you – **you must promise that their survey responses will be confidential on an individual basis** – only headlines, patterns, and trends will be shared at the meeting.

The survey questions are designed based on the goal of the meeting, but some standard questions I have used include:

- Tell me about you: How long have you been with this organization, and what is your role? *People love to help you know more about them.*
- What do you see as the strengths of this team or this organization?
- What do you see as the challenges of this team or this organization?
- What are your hopes for this retreat?
- Do you have any concerns about this retreat?
- How would you define success for this retreat?

Metric questions are great, measurable, and can be used in several ways. You can measure the pre-survey results and later conduct a post survey—say thirty to sixty days after the event is over—to show the movement. With a great session, there will be improvement, and you have just increased the value of the work you have done.

I use a scale of 1 to 5, with 5 being high. A five-point scale allows me to relate the results to the group comparing it to an A to F scale, which is very clear!

You can ask: *How would you rate how well this team*

- Works together
- Communicates
- Shares ideas
- Trusts each other
- Etc.

  (Customize the options based on the goals of the session)

When you assure people of individual confidentiality, you will be surprised at how much people will tell you. They open up quickly, feeling safe to share personal insights about themselves and stories about the function (or dysfunction) of the team and organization. And as the facilitator, you become so much better prepared for the retreat day. In fact, in many cases, you will already know more than the leader about the team's nuances, dynamics, and needs!

Typically, I will share the entire summary with verbatim comments and average scores in advance with the leader. No names are attached. This information enables me to share the "why" behind the recommended agenda design.

Another benefit of the pre-event survey is that on retreat day, the participants will feel like they already know you. They feel connected to you since they have shared their opinions with you. Now you are less of a stranger as you begin the day together.

Once all the survey results are in, your job is to headline the key findings of each question. I recommend that you share these results as a top-line summary at the retreat

DON'T SHY AWAY FROM THE TOUGH COMMENTS AND ISSUES.

The more you can put it all out on the table at the retreat and say this is what I heard in the surveys, the quicker the group will be able to get to work on solving the challenges presented.

You can use key verbatim comments (no names) as a way to synthesize what you heard.

Another option is to send the entire summarized document of all verbatim results to everyone in advance of the retreat for review. On retreat day, you then can begin with a way for them to share their own key findings.

The most successful way I have found to manage this particular process is to post flip charts on the wall with the headline "Pre-Survey Key Takeaways." As people come in, ask them to post their comments on the flip charts.

Then as a group, you can review the comments and summarize findings. This process gives people voices to start the day and allows them to begin seeing what their colleagues are thinking as well.

One of the most interesting dynamics happens when people, who think they are the only ones who feel a certain way, see similar comments. There is great reassurance in thoughts such as, "I didn't know that others thought that way too!"

I find that these surveys with the headlines presented first thing in the morning (you know they are curious) get the meeting into a productive mode right off the bat. Without the honesty of having the "this is where you are" information being shared up front, it can take several hours of people being superficially polite—with you and each other—as they try to "feel out" the room before they are put at ease. The survey information says, "Here is where you are—let's get to work."

CLIENT QUESTIONS & PRE-SURVEYS ARE THE **FIRST STEPS** FOR AN EFFECTIVE RETREAT.

WHAT TO WEAR AND NOT WEAR

Part of planning ahead involves deciding what to wear.

So consider: what kind of first impression do you want to make? Professional? Authoritative? Relaxed?

First of all, regardless of the style or formality of the event, remember that it will be a long day, so make a rule that you will be comfortable. This is another one of my painful lessons learned!

A facilitator making constant clothing adjustments or hobbling around by the end of the day because of uncomfortable shoes is not a pretty sight.

Dress one step up from your audience. Most retreats are casual, and folks will show up in jeans and even shorts. But as a facilitator, you need a certain level of professionalism to command audience attention and respect.

At the same time, don't overdo it. You want to look professional but also to fit in and blend, so know your audience. The event is about them, not you.

Wear neutrals instead of a red blazer; this is not a speaking engagement. As a mirror check, ask yourself:

"Would I want to listen to and follow this person?"

You are there to facilitate others' thinking. Be professional (think business casual, with an emphasis on business) in an understated way.

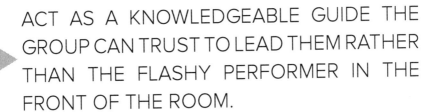

ACT AS A KNOWLEDGEABLE GUIDE THE GROUP CAN TRUST TO LEAD THEM RATHER THAN THE FLASHY PERFORMER IN THE FRONT OF THE ROOM.

CHAPTER 3
Agenda Design

Thanks to the pre-surveys, you will have a good idea of what you are walking into on the meeting day. Your agenda's design will keep you and the day on track. It serves as your personal road map and is especially critical since you are the driver for the day with a bus full of people depending on you!

For myself, I create detailed, to-the-minute agendas so I can track where we will be at any given moment and where we need to go.

However, this kind of detail is for my eyes only.

I build in flex times, knowing that the day will never go exactly as planned.

Some discussions will be shorter, and some will be longer, but with your detailed map, and the ability to think on your feet, you will keep things on schedule to achieve your goal.

For the client, I provide a simplified agenda without specific times.

I want them to be confident knowing:

- We will cover all the details.
- What the expectations are for them if they are speaking.
- They can participate rather than watch the clock or worry if a specific topic occurs five minutes later than planned.

SAMPLE—Detailed Agenda for Myself

Here's a short sample from a retreat I delivered to one of my clients:

Logistics:

- Two Post-it flip charts and two easels
- Tables pre-assigned
- Lunch ready to serve at 11:30

Draft Working Agenda—Not for Distribution:

11:30
Participants arrive (pre-assigned tables), pick up their lunches, begin eating.

11:35
David (leader) opens session, welcomes, provides a brief update on the organization and the reason for today's session. Shares his hopes for the session, introduces Mary.

11:50
Mary—icebreaker.

Working agreements for brainstorming.

12:10
At tables—brainstorm initiatives/organizations under categories.

12:40
At tables, select top three choices in each category.

12:50
Scribe on flip charts by category. Review all ideas as a large group.

1:15
Each participant votes on the top three choices from across all categories.

1:30
Break while "votes" tallied—top choices reviewed.

1:45
David—Next steps, express gratitude for their time.

2:00
Conclude.

SAMPLE—Client Agenda—For Same Session

Logistics:

- Two Post-it flip charts and two easels
- Tables pre-assigned
- Lunch ready to serve at 11:30

Draft Working Agenda—Not for Distribution:

11:30
Participants arrive (pre-assigned tables), pick up their lunches, begin eating.

David (leader) opens session, welcomes, provides a brief update on the organization and the reason for today's session. Shares his hopes for the session, introduces Mary.

11:50
Mary—icebreaker.

Working agreements for brainstorming.

At Tables:

- Brainstorming initiatives/organizations under categories
- Select their top three choices in each category
- Scribe on flip charts by category
- Review all ideas as a large group

Each participant votes on the top three choices from across all categories.

Break.

"Votes" tallied.

Top choices reviewed.

1:45
David—Next steps, express gratitude for their time.

2:00
Conclude.

I resist giving participants a paper agenda at all.

Instead, with a prepared flip chart, I talk them through a top-line overview of where we are going for the day with no specified times (other than categories for morning and afternoon).

I **really** don't want them clock watching! I want them focused on the content and how to apply it.

 NOTE:

One facilitator I spoke with has a unique way to think about agendas.

1. If **time** and achieving specific goals are most important, then draft the agenda by time frames.

2. If **topic** discussions are more important, draft agenda by topic—which will naturally show that time is less important than the actual discussion.

SAMPLE—Participant Agenda

On A Flip Chart — Same Session as Previous

- David update
- Brainstorm
- Choose top priorities
- Next steps

AGENDA DESIGN RECOMMENDATIONS

- **Start with an Icebreaker.**

    Icebreakers are a great way to infuse immediate energy (and fun) into your meeting. Learn more in the icebreakers chapter.

    PEOPLE NEED TO HEAR THE SOUND OF THEIR OWN VOICES BEFORE THEY CAN HEAR YOURS.

- **Schedule your agenda such that participants get a chance to speak/interact at least once every thirty to forty-five minutes.**

    Long presentations or downloads are deadly. If a department presentation by a company team or the leader is required, try to keep it to thirty minutes or less. If it must be longer, plan for discussion or a break, so people aren't sitting and listening for too long.

- **In a perfect world, ask to see other presentations ahead of time and try to work with presenters to ensure that their presentation (and PowerPoint) is on-point and relevant to the day (although such access is not always possible).**

    Boring speakers can drag down your meeting. Most of the time, I allocate speaker time and keep my fingers crossed, and, while listening to a speaker's presentation, I figure out how best to refocus the group when the speaker finishes and I return to facilitating.

- **Small group work is more effective than large group discussions, so create opportunities for people to interact.**

  People will be much more likely to speak their opinions in groups of two to six than in a group of ten or more. Give groups specific work to do or questions to discuss for five to twenty minutes (depending on the work) in small teams. Have them scribe and flip chart their discussions and then present their thinking to the larger group. Encourage different presenters each time to make it more interesting and engage more people. And here's a tip: encourage the top organizational leaders not to present; they are heard from all the time.

- **Plan a morning and an afternoon break.**

  Tell people they have ten minutes, but plan for fifteen. Be ready to make adjustments based on body language; you may need to give a break earlier than planned if you start to lose people. You will know this is happening if you see that people are getting fidgety or starting a one-by-one parade leaving and returning to the room. Managing breaks is a bit like herding cats. Most people are pretty compliant, and you are best served by keeping the agenda moving. Don't worry about the inevitable stragglers. I always plan something immediately after the break that is interesting but not critical for everyone to be in the room, just in case.

- **Even with the best facilitation, plan a caffeine and sugar break for the afternoon.**

  The "after lunch" blues can set in, and a food/snack break does wonders. Afternoon cookies are a meeting staple!

- **For a full day, I recommend ending by 4:00 pm.**

  Most groups begin to get comatose by late afternoon. All this thinking and interacting is hard work! And if you tell them you will end at 4:00 pm, don't be surprised if at 3:45 p.m., people are looking at their watches. If you really want to be their hero, exceed expectations and end five or ten minutes early. At all costs, avoid going past the scheduled end time. Participants' love and support of you will dissipate quickly if the meeting goes long!

- **Mornings typically provide the maximum level of creative energy (especially after the coffee).**

  Find common ground for the group to start strong first thing in the meeting. Showing their summarized responses to the surveys is a great way to demonstrate that they have more in common than different.

- **Team building exercises and development bring the group together creating their common purpose, vision, and team values.**

  Build trust before you jump into more controversial discussions as the day unfolds.

- **Be sure to do one final check-in call several days before the event to be sure all is as was discussed.**

  Recently, I was booked to facilitate a three-hour session with thirty-six people to develop an organizational service culture for one specific team. The design was complete and the agenda included work sessions for six small groups to roll up their sleeves and develop new service culture standards. I suggested a check-in call four days before the event. The call went something like this:

> **Me** - "I'm looking forward to the session next week and just wanted to check in with you to be sure we are all set for the day as we discussed."

> **Response** - "Yes, we are all set; just one small change...instead of thirty-six people, we have expanded the invitation to more departments, and we now have one hundred thirty attendees, so we will be meeting in an auditorium."

> **Me** (*long and deep breath*) - "Okay. With the larger group, I will need to make a few adjustments to the agenda and the expected outcomes. This program will now be less about creating detailed plans and more about introducing the material with follow-up discussions."

> **Response:** "That sounds great!"

Gulp —Truthfully, the agenda needed to be totally revised. My Plan B was a redesign wherein those in the auditorium would choose three people around them to create informal, small groups for the purpose of discussing the topics throughout the morning. It worked wonderfully, but my original agenda went out the window.

Such is the life of a facilitator; you always need to be light on your feet – *and never let them see you sweat!*

CHAPTER 4
Planning Icebreakers

Icebreakers can be fun and powerful to set the tone for the day—or silly and irritating (setting a quite different tone for the day). In this chapter, we'll explore how to ensure your icebreakers are working for you and not against you. A friend of mine calls hers "Opening Connections" which is a great way to explain the purpose behind the exercise.

KEYS FOR PICKING MEANINGFUL ICEBREAKERS

- **Ask yourself: would you want to do it?**

  Some icebreakers are pretty awful. I've read through hundreds of icebreaker ideas and shudder when I think about trying to do such silly games with professional groups! Icebreakers such as giving each person a playing deck card and asking them to combine for the best poker hand (what happens if people don't know how to play?) or designing your own tombstone (kind of a morbid way to start) are a calculated risk and should only be used if you know the group well.

- **Have you tried the icebreaker?**

  Practice makes perfect. It's not wise to try it out on a group for your first time implementing it. Try it on your family or friends if you have to; they will be brutally honest if it is too complicated or meaningless.

he icebreaker fit the audience?

Consider the male/female mix, age, and industry when choosing icebreakers. Icebreakers that you plan for a group of construction workers should be different than for a group of HR professionals. Depending on the audience, some icebreakers are very elementary or too warm and fuzzy, such as share a deep, dark secret that nobody in the whole wide world knows or bring in a baby picture (inevitably, some will forget). If the audience perceives the icebreaker as a waste of time, it can damage your credibility for knowing how to motivate them and reduce trust in you to lead them for the rest of the day.

- **Does the icebreaker have a point?**

    Tie the icebreaker to the focus or theme of the day, so there is continuity in your agenda design. Ensure that there is a correlation between what you are doing in the icebreaker and what you want to accomplish for the day — validating the why for the activity.

    IDEALLY, THE ICEBREAKER NEEDS TO HAVE A PURPOSE AND NOT JUST BE AN ACTIVITY.

- **Tap into resources.**

    There are plenty of good ideas on the Internet these days. I have purchased several useful books in the *Games Trainers Play* series by McGraw-Hill Training. Trainers Warehouse also has lots of tools (although some are on the silly side).

LOGISTICS FOR ICEBREAKERS

- **Make sure you have everything you need for the icebreaker and are not dependent on the venue or client.**

  For example, many venues say they have markers, but they forget to mention that they are thin, running dry, the color yellow, or are white-board markers.

- **Make directions for the icebreaker easy and clear.**

  Put the directions on a flip chart or PowerPoint slide if necessary. You do not want groups floundering, calling out "what are we supposed to do?" or doing the exercise incorrectly and being embarrassed as a result.

- **Tap into the competitive spirit.**

  Lots of groups get charged by competitive icebreakers. Make yours fun. Prizes are optional; bragging rights are normally all they need!

- **Use thick, colored markers.**

  Blue and green are my favorite colors. They have a great readability and add a little personality and energy to the discussion. These colors definitely make things more lively than a black marker. On the other hand, red reminds me of corrections on my school papers growing up or the business phrase "in the red" so it is not a positive color to see splashed all over the retreat room.

  Don't ask me why marker packages even bother to come with yellow, since yellow can't be seen by most participants.

ICEBREAKERS THAT ALWAYS WORK WELL

Two-minute introductions for group members to get to know each other better.

- Equipment required: none
- Here are the facilitated four steps:

  1. Have individuals pair up. Invite everyone to stand and select a person they don't know very well.

  2. In pairs, have them decide who will go first.

  3. The first person must talk about himself/herself—history, life, family, hobbies, dreams—for two minutes while the other person stays silent and listens. As the facilitator, you time the two minutes and tell everyone when to switch.

  4. At the end of the second two-minute period, have everyone remain standing, and ask each person to share with the larger group one thing that he/she learned about his/her partner. Interesting things come out; people are amazed about what they didn't know and have great laughs to start the day.

Another fun and very easy "get to know you" activity is to go around the room and have people share how they got their first and/or middle names.

- Equipment required: none
- Facilitation—around the room or in small groups.
- Most have interesting stories, and it helps people learn something about their peers—that perhaps they are real people with stories and not just possibly irritating cube-mates.

PERCEPTIONS ACTIVITY

Equipment:

Eyedroppers, Nickels, Small Cups of Water, and Napkins
(One of each per table.)

Follow these steps:

1. Divide people into small groups of four to six per table.

2. Show everyone an eyedropper and a nickel, and ask them as a table group to determine how many drops of water from the eyedropper to the nickel they think it will take before the water flows off the nickel.

3. Take guesses from each table **before** you give them the supplies. Groups have been known to start the activity before being asked! Typically, the guesses will be five to ten drops. Create a flip chart with two to three columns.

   Column one—Pre-guesses, by table

   Column two —Actual for round one, by table

   Column three—Actual for round two, by table

   (optional)

   Scribe on the flip chart in column one the pre-guesses of each table.

   Note: every once in a while, someone will have done the activity, so ask that person to allow the others to enjoy the learning moment.

4. Give each table an eyedropper, nickel, cup of water, and a napkin to help them determine when the water overflows. Have each group place the nickel (heads up) on the napkin and use the eyedropper to drop water onto the nickel. Ask them to count how many drops it holds until it overflows. (It's typically twenty to forty.) Scribe numbers by table in column two.

5. Most are very surprised by the difference in how many drops they thought the nickel could hold (column one) versus the total drops the nickel did hold (column two).

6. An option is to repeat the exercise for them to see again (now that they have a better understanding of what can happen).

7. **The debrief:** Sometimes (even as smart professionals), our perceptions about something or someone may be wrong. You can share that perhaps they came to this meeting with some assumptions, some of which might be wrong. The message behind this is to ask them to please keep an open mind for the rest of the day about what may be possible to achieve.

CHAPTER 5
Room Set-Up and Logistics

As you prepare, determine what equipment you may need, and consider buying the equipment you can't live without. Despite your best-laid plans, know that every engagement may bring surprises. "Oh sure, we have a flip chart easel" can mean it's old, damaged, and doesn't stand up. Ancient equipment exists in many companies. Remember, ultimately all of these details reflect on you.

It is important to let the meeting planner you are working with know your expected logistics.

These logistics include:

- Recommended room set up—how you specifically want this room to look.
- Request for table set-up—small group tables for four to six people, a U shaped table, a conference table, etc.
- Number of flip charts (*and easels*).
- Pens and pads on the tables.
- Small table up front for all your materials.
- Projector and screen (*if using PowerPoint*).
- Your agenda timing—such as morning break, lunch, and afternoon cookie break.

It goes without saying (*or does it?*) to arrive at least an hour early. Typically, even with the list above clearly communicated, things are not going to be set up as you planned (*yet another reason to be in comfortable clothes*).

YOU MIGHT WANT TO PLAN ON:

- Moving tables so ideally there are four to six people per table.
- Making sure there are pens and pads of paper for all participants.
- Tracking down AV guys.
- Setting up your PowerPoint and flip charts.
- Dragging a table up front for your supplies.
- Preparing your flip charts (*or you can do this in advance*)—with work for the day such as the agenda overview.

YOU WILL NEED TO LOCATE:

- The room thermostat, or find out how to adjust the temperature. (*Chances are it will be too hot or too cold at some point during the day, and people will come to you.*)
- The light controls.
- The restrooms. (*You will be asked.*)
- The contact at the facility who will be available in case questions arise during the day.

Let your participants see a relaxed, confident, and fully prepared facilitator (not one fussing, sweating, and fuming with how to get the projector working or fumbling with how to set up an easel).

When your client/leader arrives, specifically reach out to this person to touch base for the day. I recommend that the client be the one to open the retreat. Also, assure the client he or she can touch base with you (*preferably on break*) if there are questions or comments about the discussion or the plan throughout the day.

One good practice for both you and the client leader is to try to get around to shake hands and greet everyone in the room—work the room, as they say. If you've made that connection, people will be more ready to hear what you have to say.

YOUR GOAL IS TO BE FULLY PREPARED

so you are set and ready to welcome even the first, early participants when they arrive. Think of yourself as a host greeting your dinner guests.

CHAPTER 6
Kick Off the Day

The client leader should kick off the day (with your pre-discussed personal coaching on message points) to welcome, express appreciation for everyone being there, state their hopes for the day, and introduce you with the goal of keeping it short and sweet.

Lesson learned: know that the "five to ten minutes" that you have allocated to the leader in your agenda could consume a larger block of time. Don't let this get you off your game. If you do (and I have), you begin the day in a frazzled state of mind, because you think you are already behind. This has thrown me for a loop a couple of times, but it goes into the learning bucket of that which you cannot control. Know that you can always make timing adjustments throughout the session (especially since you are the only one with the detailed agenda).

Another challenge in the opening is having a leader who is not so beloved by his/her team. In that case, know that even the kick-off messages can take the air out of the room. If this is the case (and you will know in advance based on the pre-surveys), part of your agenda design needs to include a recovery plan to restore the positive energy and get your participants engaged.

Some recovery plans are:
- using your icebreaker or adding another one.
- doing an around-the-room of "share what you like best about this company (or team)."
- taking a break—although it may be a little early.

YOUR INTRODUCTION

Although I provide bios on request, I always prefer that the client introduce me based on how he/she knows me. I find long bios read verbatim incredibly boring as a listener—and often a bit pompous.

GETTING STARTED

Once introduced, start by smiling. Come across as warm and confident to position yourself as a partner on the journey. Don't come across as any of these:

- A high-pitched, overly enthusiastic kindergarten teacher:

    "Good mooorrrning, Ladies and Gentlemen— we are going to have soooo much fun today!"

- High-powered motivational speaker:
    "SO—ARE YOU READY TO CHANGE THE WORLD TODAY?"

- A cozy best friend:
    "I'm sure you all don't really want to be here this morning—let me tell you what happened to ME last night."

- A stern, no-nonsense drill sergeant:
    "Okay, Folks, we've got a LOT of WORK to do today— so I EXPECT everyone's FULL cooperation, or we will be here LONG past the ending time—GOT IT?"

I've experienced all of the above, and none of them endear the facilitator to me. You have seven seconds to make a first impression.

Think and plan what you are going to say first and *rehearse, rehearse, rehearse*. Consider: How will you welcome the group? How will you connect to the group? What have past facilitators done that helped usher you into a good frame of mind to begin the day?

> Share the abbreviated agenda on a flip chart or PowerPoint slide. Be sure to include breaks and lunch (sadly, the most important parts of the day for some in the room). Remember, don't list specific times other than to state what will happen in the morning versus afternoon.
>
> As people arrive, I let everyone come in and sit wherever they like (typically with their friends). I explain that I am going to move them around to gain some new perspectives. I then count off around the room (based on the number of tables) and move them to new tables.
>
> They may be unhappy with you at first, but I've had many groups tell me that this was one of the best parts of the day. If you feel the energy is getting stale, do it again after lunch; it forces participants to interact with new groups of people, and the ensuing discussions are much richer.

Often, I enjoy starting the meeting by acknowledging that there are four types of people in the room (and that all are okay). I know I have personally been each of these at different meetings throughout my career.

types are:

- **Hostages** – They feel they must endure the day as punishment.

- **Vacationers** – They don't care what we do—they are away from the office, and that's a great thing!

- **Critics** – They won't like anything—the bagels, the marker colors, the room.

- **Learners** – They are truly interested in what they might learn and are ready to try to make it a productive day.

Even as I share these four types, people will smile, and you'll hear nervous laughter—proof positive that they see themselves in these definitions—and everyone can relax since I've acknowledged that what they are feeling is common.

I have also found that in every team and organization there is a **DDO**, the "Designated Difficult One." They won't be hard to find. The key is to identify them and manage them as best you can but know you will not be able to convert them in one retreat. Read on for more ways to manage them.

With most groups, especially those whose members have some challenges with one another, I start by asking, "What working agreements will make this a productive day and worth your time?"

The typical answers include:
(*sometimes after a pause and a slow start*)

- *Being honest*
- *Staying open to others' ideas*
- *Listening well*
- *Having "fun"*
  (*It surprises me how often I need to suggest this one!*)
- *And I always add my final agreement, stating that although I would love to have the ability to read minds, I cannot, so "silence is consent." I have to trust that if they do not agree with something that is being said (especially if they have honesty in the grouping), they will speak up. I then ask if they will abide by these agreements this day. Usually this is met with silence, and I say, "Great—silence is consent"—which gets a laugh.*

The beginning of the day is also a great place to start to manage those who speak loudly (and long) while others remain quiet. (*More on this in the next chapter*)

CHAPTER 7
Skills and Challenges

There have been times when I've initially been intimidated by my audiences. When I have facilitated a group of doctors, professors, or ministers, I have sometimes second-guessed myself on what I have planned. However, even though I may not have a medical degree, PhD, or Masters of Divinity, I do know how to get a group of people (yes, they are real people) to work together to solve problems.

It is important to have confidence in your facilitation skills regardless of the audience. I have found that all groups of people are more similar than different when it comes to their lack of love for meetings and their secret hope that this one just might be productive.

Groups feed off your energy. They will match you if your energy is low and be energized when it is high. (**Caution:** Make sure your facilitator energy is not over the top. I've seen some scary, HIGHLY energized facilitators who make you want to shut down and hide or wish you could find an "off" button somewhere.)

People love to see their words written down. Summarize as they speak and flip chart their responses. It is affirming and validating for them to see their words on a flip chart. Ask each person if you captured their thoughts correctly. Learn to write clearly and quickly. If someone gives you a run-on sentence, ask them how you can best capture their thought in a few words.

Writing quickly can sometimes lead to misspellings. In a fast moving brainstorm, when you are scribing as fast as you can, your brain can freeze as mine has with words like camaraderie, pneumonia, entrepreneurial, or my personal favorite, Albuquerque. I solve this by showing a spell check symbol at the top of the flip chart and promising that all spellings will be corrected when I prepare the final report.

Sometimes, you may get topics or comments out of left field. They are not on the agenda for the day but it is important not to ignore them. Tell and show the participants that you will start a "Parking Lot" flip chart to capture these comments, and include them in the follow-up notes for future discussion.

It's important to learn to stay relaxed with (short) rabbit trails and the inevitable room comedians—those dying to get a laugh. They can be a tension reliever for the group, so don't let them become a stress producer for you.

The more people have a chance to talk, the more people will warm up to you and feel engaged—which ensures that they are buying into their work and the goals for the day.

Ensure your agenda has plenty of participant talk time.

TIPS FOR FACILITATING DISCUSSION

- **In small to medium sized groups (*with ten to thirty members*), ask a question and go around the room so that everyone has a chance to answer.** Ask each person to respond in one word or one sentence so the answers don't drag on. Use questions such as:

- What do you hope is accomplished today?
- What surprised you most about that discussion or presentation?
- How do you feel about the work accomplished this morning?
- How are you feeling about the work accomplished so far today?

- **Small group work always ensures more energy and discussion.** Help them with a fun way to get started such as:

  - The person with the shortest hair starts

  - The person who has been there the longest (*or shortest*) starts.

  - Everyone at the table points their index fingers skyward, and on the count of three, they point at whomever at their table they think should start.

  - Make sure they assign a "*scriber*" who has readable writing and a presenter who will share with the larger group.

CLEAR DIRECTIONS FOR SMALL GROUPS

I always know I have done this well when I DON'T get asked questions such as, "What were we supposed to do?"

I've been most successful when I:

- Tell the groups ahead of time how much time they will have to discuss. I may give them fifteen minutes with twenty minutes in the schedule.

- Tell them in advance that they need to choose a scribe and speaker to present their work. The speaker should change each time, rather than be the same person all day. And ideally, the organizational leaders should let others step up.

- Give groups a maximum of three questions to discuss and flip chart. More than three questions drag the group down, typically causing them to get stuck and not finish. It is important for people to feel successful throughout the day.

- Design a PowerPoint slide with the three questions, or post the three questions on a flip chart, so everyone can continue to see (and be reminded of) what they are supposed to be doing.

- Pre-prepare a flip chart sheet for each small group, with the three questions as headings, so all they have to do is fill in the blanks. This method also makes it simple for you to type up the notes later since every group has the same template.

When small groups present and you want feedback from all the groups, here's an effective two-step process to follow:

First, ask the group at large to start with a round of what "I LIKE" about the group's ideas.

- *Share positives of the ideas*
- *Affirm the thinking*
- *Build on the thought processes*

The second feedback round should be stated in terms of "I WISH." This allows new ideas or dissenting opinions to be presented or added to the discussion in a helpful matter.

- *I wish the ideas included ...*
- *I wish we could find more inexpensive ways to solve the issue ...*
- *I wish one department didn't have to carry the whole load ...*

This "I like" and "I wish" is a highly structured exchange and feedback session, and to be honest, some of my most highly educated and experienced clients at first bristle at this type of format. They are more familiar with their usual free-for-all pile-on with the things that are wrong. These groups come to love the "I like" and "I wish" process as they see that it encourages positive and negative feedback while keeping the meetings productive and positive.

KEEP THEM MOVING

Throughout the day, it is important for people to stay engaged in the discussions. Physically moving around helps with this. Movement can include several of the following ideas:

- Counting off and changing tables.

- Having groups flip chart their small group discussions and then present their findings, utilizing one person as a speaker or allowing them to report as a group.

- Moving around physically to show their choices or different opinions on flip charts around the room. Use the four corners of the room with a flip chart (and topic) in each corner, and have them physically go to their choice corner. They enjoy the movement and seeing who else shows up in their particular corner.

- Posting flip charts on the walls around the room, each with a headline, and giving participants markers to write their thoughts or ideas on all the charts. Participants can walk around and write comments with their markers (ensure you have enough markers for everyone).

- "Voting" on concepts on a flip chart. Round color-coding labels at office supply stores work well. I give each person three dots (colors do not have any significance) and ask them to make their choices. When the "polls close," I count up the dots per choice, and we discuss the outcomes as a group.

- Securing adjacent rooms for small group discussions. This is great for creating fresh space and thinking; but as a facilitator, you will rack up your walking miles to check up on them and then round up the troops. Did I mention to be sure you are in comfortable clothes and shoes?

- Ensuring breaks, and ideally a lunch out of the meeting room for a change of scenery. Although keep in mind that the wider the area the group inhabits, the more of a "herding cats" mentality you may encounter when you need to get them to return and get refocused.

FOLLOW-UP TEAMS

For additional follow-up work (and to keep the momentum of the day's work), you may want to create new committees or teams to continue to solve challenges raised in the meeting and I recommend letting people do the following:

Own the decisions. People stay engaged on follow-up teams much longer if the following four conditions exist:

1. **They have created the need for the teams and prioritized the team topics.**

   In the last part of the day, there may be a list of key issues requiring team follow up. Allow the team to choose the top ones that they want to tackle (include any the team leader considers mandatory). Based on the number of retreat participants, try to get the topics down to four to six so that your participants can begin the process of solving issues.

2. **Each participant gets to choose his or her team.**

Let's say there are four topics for follow-up work. Set up one topic in each corner of the room. Let participants know that on the count of three, they are to go to the corner/topic of their choice and that everyone must participate on one team. Try to evenly divide your participant population by telling them that if there are too many people in one corner, a willing party should pick their second choice.

3. **Each team has a clear stated goal and short time frame—thirty days to three months is ideal.**

Once participants have chosen their teams, give these new teams thirty to forty minutes to have their first meeting and to flip chart their work.

Their first team meeting agenda should include:

- Brainstorm ideas and solutions.

- Choose one or two of the brainstormed ideas to move forward.

- Identify their time frames—what will be done by when within the agreed general time frame.

- Identify who's on their team (could add others not in the room).

- Identify co-chairs (at least one of these must be in the room at the start). I find co-chairs are more effective for sharing the load, keeping the group moving, and keeping the team approach.

4. **For accountability, recommend that these new teams provide regular updates at staff meetings.** (Some teams will move faster than others but a little healthy competition is a good thing.)

Keep all flip charted team presentations in the retreat notes to give each committee a real head-start to accomplish their goals as a team rather than leaving the retreat with the weak promise of "find a time to get together"—which we know will not happen.

MANAGING OTHER PRESENTERS

If other speakers are presenting, it's ideal if you can review their information ahead of time (so you can be sure the content doesn't derail the meeting). Here are three ideas for ensuring that speakers remain an asset and not a liability to your event:

- **Tell them how much time they have to speak ahead of time.** At the event, stand at the back of the room so they can see you behind the participants. As you listen and time them, hold up signs to indicate how much time they have left—five minutes, two minutes, one minute, and Time's Up!

- **When it is time for them to end, slowly walk to the front.** It is a quiet way to signal "time to wrap up," and they get the idea that they need to wind down. If they keep going, continue to reduce the distance between you and them so that ultimately you are standing next to them and ready to wrap up (when they take a breath) and move on.

- **Be prepared.** I've had speakers go on and on (which was my fault for not knowing what they would be presenting), and I needed to recover the energy and the momentum of the room when that presentation ended. Have a means of bringing the energy back up if you know that participants will be experiencing a low-energy session (even if it is an extra break).

Always have a sense of what you will cut when you find you have less time than planned and what you could add with more time. Sometimes my timed activities have gone extremely quickly. I end up thinking, "How will I fill the time now?" Be sure you always have "just in case" activities or discussions, or you can decide that ending early is not a bad thing.

BE AWARE OF FACILITATION CHALLENGES

Be a student of the facilitation—and learn what doesn't work.

- I've learned to watch out for long "sitting periods." If the group gets restless, I create an on-the-spot activity to get people moving around.

- I've learned to make small group instructions simple and clear so the exercises will be effective and stay within their time boundaries.

- I've learned to manage my own reactions (and facial expressions) when someone was getting under my skin.

- I've learned there are times to insert an opinion and times not to insert an opinion.

- I've learned that sometimes it's necessary to back off of a position that I feel is logical and find a new way to proceed.

Never let them see you sweat. Never show irritation or defensiveness at any comment. If you realize you are irritated, chances are everyone in the room already can see it on your face and hear it in your tone.

THE PARTICIPANTS ARE WATCHING YOU LIKE HAWKS.

You lose credibility if you allow someone to get under your skin. You must maintain control of the room and the discussion.

- I was once working with a church; they wanted lots of extra discussion, and we were getting way off schedule. One of the leaders asked me for more time in a small group work session. I was getting frustrated with their pace, so I said not so graciously, "So how much time do you want?" My not-so-gracious response stung as I thought about it later, and I have regretted it ever since.

- There are often negative retreat participants who seem to be focused on being contrary to whatever the discussion. They may be driving you crazy, but your face must show a calm, smiling, and attentive expression while gently guiding the discussion back on track.

REMEMBER THAT AS A FACILITATOR, **you know where you are going for the day and how you will get there. The participants in the room are along for the ride; but they are not driving, so it can be uncomfortable for them.**

Be patient and know that by the end of the day, the participants will understand the 'why' behind the day and the activities, and all will be well again.

They just have to "trust" this perfect stranger—you—and hope it is not a wasted day.

Be okay with interruptions or requests to double back on an issue.

I've learned that I need to make sure MY agenda doesn't become THE agenda for the meeting. Again, watch your body language and tone. Be able to flex with the group while ensuring that you stay on time and on track. Sometimes major portions of an agenda may need to change; the key is to keep your focus on the ultimate goal for the day and know that there is more than one road to get you there. I have often used breaks or lunchtime to recalibrate based on where we are and where we need to go to ensure that we stay on task. (Bring a Power Bar as you likely may not be eating lunch.)

Know that some groups are passive (and you wish they would get more passionate) and some are SO passionate, it is hard to rein them in and stay on task.

I've learned to love both and adjust my style to help them move forward.

YOU ARE THERE TO FACILITATE, not to solve their problem; it is theirs to solve.

Keep a light/humorous attitude that does not let the conversation get derailed. When rabbit trails start to form, here are a couple solutions:

- Let a conversation go for a few minutes—even if it is totally off topic. Then, introduce a "Parking Lot" flip chart for important ideas that may or may not get solved that day. At least, people will feel their ideas are captured and will be in the notes for further discussion.

- For someone (let's say John) who dominates the conversation, suggest:

  - *"John has some great points. I'd like to hear from others."*
  - *"John, I'd like to summarize and capture what you are saying on a flip chart; can you give me the headline?"*
  - *If it is a topic that will be covered later, suggest, "John, you are right on track, and we are going to spend more time on that topic later today; please don't let me forget your ideas on this topic."*

AND TALKING TOO MUCH INCLUDES THE FACILITATOR. Throughout the day, insert your personal opinions extremely sparingly. Your role is not to convince, but to facilitate discussion. This can be a real challenge if you feel like you have the answers for them, but hold your tongue and let *them* work it out.

I am not a fan of handouts at a retreat. The process of handling paper and reading handouts lowers engagement (when heads are down reading, they are not engaged). Minimal handouts are okay, but keep them absolutely minimal. If you do use handouts, plan for the following to occur around distribution:

- There will be noise and commotion in the distribution process, so don't try to speak over the activity.

- People will be reading what has just been handed to them, so know that you will lose them for several minutes.

- No one is listening when things are being handed out.

- Suggestion: hand out packets per table over a break to ease the process.

Speaking of heads down, reading body language is key for a facilitator. By looking across the room, you know who is engaged and who is not.

Signs of the disengagement are:

- Sitting with crossed arms
- Slouching in their seats
- Looking at cell phones
- Talking with neighbors
- Showing that bored look in their eyes

When I first started facilitating, there were days when I would spend 80 percent of my energy trying to get a non-engaged participant to "get with the spirit." Doing so usually didn't work and was exhausting. These days, I make note of who those people are and perhaps try to connect with them on a break. But I accept the fact that 80 percent of the room IS "getting it" and that either the non-engaged will come along or write off the day.

I'D RATHER FOCUS MY ENERGY ON THOSE WHO WILL MAKE A DIFFERENCE.

True confession: Body language reading is not always accurate. I've had what I think are some of the most negative people in the room provide the most positive feedback at the end, creating a lesson learned not to assume you always know what people are thinking.

When there are clear conflicts of opinion in the room, remain as the mediator (*even if you have an opinion*). The best approach is to validate the legitimacy of each opinion, seek to understand what each person is saying, capture each idea clearly for the notes, and possibly add the issue to the *"Parking Lot"* chart for future discussion and decisions, unless it requires more discussion then and there.

Recently, when I was facilitating a small retreat, an influential individual spoke harshly to those in the room, taking all the air out of the discussion. It was important to process the comments calmly (by asking for clarification and reactions from those in the room) and then to revise the agenda (both that day and the next morning) to deal with the issue appropriately before we could move forward.

In managing difficult personalities, you can match them at their game. I've had healthy discussions going with a large group, when someone would comment under his or her breath (which I would overhear), "That'll never happen."

I will share with the group, "(Name) doesn't think that will ever happen; do others agree?"

I follow the nine seconds of silence rule after a facilitated question to get people to respond. To you, it may seem like an eternity, but if you stay quiet, someone will speak!

It is important that you are perceived as a calm facilitator who accepts differences in opinion, even if they are disagreeing with you! There will always be diverse points of view, and participants have to know it is okay to disagree with you or anyone else.

It is good to remember that some will not like you for whatever reason and that others may not like the direction of the day (or a host of other objections). Most of the objections are not about you, and you still have to drive to the goal and objective for the day.

Be okay with questions like "Why are we doing this?" "What did you say?" or "Instead of your directions, can we do it this way?" Instead of feeling that they are being difficult or not paying attention, I've learned that they may have a point, and I can adjust. If small groups have to ask repeatedly what the assignment is, then I haven't done a good job in communicating. Yet another lesson for me, and perhaps new ideas for next time.

If two people consistently are talking to one another as an aside, give them a sincere smile and graciously invite them to share their discussion with everyone. This is a sure-fire way to curtail the sidebars.

DEALING WITH EVER-PRESENT CELL PHONES

An upfront reminder to mute cellphones is always a good idea with the promise of breaks to check messages.

I've seen some facilitators use different ways to deal with a cell phone ringing, such as having music for someone to dance to if their phone goes off. I haven't used this technique, as I believe it could be mortifying for some and completely shut them down for the rest of the meeting.

One great example was a facilitator who responded when a phone rang, "Thanks for the reminder—please everyone turn off your cell phones." Cell phone use also varies by industry. I've become more accustomed to the use in healthcare (it could be a real medical emergency) and know that cell phone use has become a necessary evil that facilitators cannot completely control.

OTHER THINGS TO CONSIDER

Another difference among facilitators is the use of music played during work times or thought times. I've tried it without much success. Either it is too quiet to make any difference, too loud and interruptive as people work, or the wrong type of music for everyone's tastes. So I simply let the conversation be the "music" of the day.

If someone has a run-on point, some ways to manage it are to ask:

- How can I headline your thought on the flip chart?
- Can you give me a few words so I can capture your point?
- If I were to summarize your comments this way, does that cover it?

If someone disagrees with a point, find a positive way to state his or her concern on the flip chart.

Sometimes you just have to cut your losses. I've been with some fairly unprofessional groups. Their leader is disengaged. Participants arrive late, are immersed looking down at their phones, don't listen to you or anyone else in the room, and leave early. This hints at a much bigger cultural issue. Just accomplish what you can, and live to facilitate another day. However, be sure to gently mention this observation and "opportunity" in your recap summary.

CHAPTER 8
Love/Hate PowerPoint

PEOPLE WILL REMEMBER:

- 10 PERCENT ORAL ALONE
- 20 PERCENT VISUAL ALONE
- 80 PERCENT VISUAL AND ORAL

(Source: Jerome Bruner, as cited by Paul Martin Lester in his article "Syntactic Theory of Visual Communication")

Lester, M.L. (2006). Syntactic Theory of Visual Communication. Cal State University of Fullerton website. http://commfaculty.fullerton.edu/lester/writings/viscomtheory.html

PowerPoint: People either love it or hate it. We've all seen the best and worst examples of PowerPoint presentations. As a facilitator, I often use PowerPoint slides because I believe people learn in different ways, and the visual reinforcement can be helpful—but I have some helpful guidelines.

- Bring your own technology. You can be caught if you have a Mac and they are set for a PC. I have learned (the hard way) to carry my own laptop, video adapter, and wireless slide advancer. If you use video in your PowerPoint, it is better to have it embedded than to rely on local wireless connections.

- PowerPoint slides should only be used as a billboard behind you to support or illustrate your points. Fewer words are the goal; too much information makes people read the slides and not pay attention to what you are saying. In my Disney marketing days, our rule of thumb for a billboard was no more than seven words. I've always enjoyed critiquing billboards on whether or not they could get their message across to a consumer like me who was going sixty miles an hour. The seven-word strategy for a billboard works for PowerPoint every time.

- Ensure that each PowerPoint slide is concise, appealing, and uses five bullet points or fewer. Wisdom has it that people cannot concentrate on more than five bullet points...*unless, of course, you're reading this book!*

- Use large type—select sizes 32+.

- Ensure readable colors and backgrounds.

- Use relevant pictures—not too cutesy (go easy on the babies, animals, and smiley faces). Once again, know your audience. I have some favorite shots I use; however, I always think through the audience—both for the type of pictures and the look of the people in the pictures. People want to see people who look like them.

- Only use short videos—ideally under five minutes—to reinforce a point. In your PowerPoint, you can add links (be sure of copyrights), but be certain to test the links. It sure can be embarrassing to fumble as you try to access the links in front of an audience.

- For training, I prefer videos that are fifteen minutes or less with discussion to follow—unless you are prepared to serve popcorn or allow some participants to get a quick nap.

- Cartoons can be fun if appropriate. They are always tricky though, because what is hilarious to you may or may not go over with your group.

- Use a PowerPoint slide to show the instructions for a small group discussion and no more than three questions to discuss.

- Activate the Girl Scout and Boy Scout motto: **Be Prepared.**

- Be ready to proceed without your PowerPoint. Think about how you would facilitate this day without your slide deck. I was once well into the day with my well-designed PowerPoint when the power went off.

So there we were in the darkened room—which also started to get quite warm. But as they say— on with the show! I continued to facilitate, in the dim light, and we made the best of it.

CHAPTER 9

Managing Your "Client"

The leader is your ultimate client. As we've explored, it is critical to know his or her definition of success right up front and ensure you deliver the outcome—in their very words—which I also include in the contract and the summary.

During the retreat, my coaching to a leader includes:

- It's important the top leader be there early to greet, stay for the entire session, and kick off and close the day with affirmation for the team and for the day.

- Other than the kick-off, for all other discussions, the leader should be the last one to speak. If the leader speaks first and articulates a position on an issue, it may likely constrict the rest of the discussion because many may feel the leader has given "the right answer."

- The leader should feel free to provide me feedback throughout the day if a topic needs to be revisited or we need to go deeper into it.

- The leader should help ensure that the organization's leadership is mixed among all tables. You don't want to create the "leader table" and have everyone else feel second-class.

- As I have previously mentioned, I strongly suggest that the organization leaders at each table not take the lead in the conversations. Let others step into these roles. Perhaps a leader can take the role of scribe and serve the others at the table. Having leaders at each table will provide great feedback at the next executive staff meeting of how conversations went at the tables—great feedback to leadership!

- The top leader should not be at any table, but should circulate among all of them to hear from all tables and be visible to all participants.

- The top leader closes the day with appreciation for the group; recognition and appreciation of a great day's work, time, and energy; and a commitment to keep the momentum moving forward. Think of this as the "motivational coach in the locker room before the big game" talk when they "break" to return to the normal workday "field."

CHAPTER 10
Finish Strong

At the end of the meeting, my favorite way to have a feel-good positive wrap-up is to provide index cards and ask everyone in the room to write down:

- One key takeaway from the meeting
- One commitment they will make going forward

Ask them to write clearly and add their names. Then have everyone go one-by-one around the room and share out loud what they have written. Collect their responses to add to the report notes which will foster built-in accountability, particularly around the commitments.

The leader should be the last to speak, share his or her responses, affirm the team, and close the meeting.

Stay engaged as people leave. Once again, consider the analogy of hosting a dinner party; spend time with people and affirm them as they leave the room.

Be sure to gather up all supplies and flip charts. One of my more embarrassing episodes with a new client was when everyone had left after a full day retreat, I quickly gathered up what I thought was everything, threw it in the trunk of my car, and headed the hour across town.

When I arrived at the FedEx office to ship my flip charts for typing, I realized I did not have the entire day's worth of flip charts.

In a heart-pounding panic, I called the facility. It was after six p.m., so of course, everyone had gone home. I called the leader and meeting planner on their cell phones to see if they had the charts. No, they did not, and I'm sure both thought I was a little ditsy and disorganized.

With despair setting in, my husband suggested we go back to the facility and try to recover them. I thought it was going to be a complete waste of time, but I had no other options.

After an hour drive back across town in the rain, in rush hour traffic, as expected, the doors to the conference center were locked. And despite vigorous knocking, there was no one home. Since it was a Friday evening, I knew that by Monday the flip charts would be long gone. In one last idea of desperation, my husband suggested checking the dumpsters for garbage from the day. I wish you could have seen us "dumpster diving" for flip charts in the rain.

I considered it a glorious success to find the flip charts covered with ketchup and mustard. It was a messy typing job for the follow-up report but I gained another classic facilitator story.

After typing up your flip charts (hopefully without ketchup on them), your written meeting summary should include:

- The names of all the participants who attended.
- The goals of success that the leader articulated.
- A summarized agenda so they remember the flow of the day.
- All flip chart notes and action steps summarized.
- Their takeaways and commitments.
- Your observations and recommendations to the group as the objective facilitator. (Which may include additional next steps for your next engagement!)
- Follow-up suggestions so they can assess how things are going.

LIFE AS A
FACILITATOR

MY TOP TEN KEYS TO SUCCESSFUL FACILITATION

1. Love a challenge (if the issues weren't hard to solve, they wouldn't need you).

2. Listen to what is (and is not) being said by your client. A little intuition goes a long way toward understanding what your client really wants and needs.

3. Understand and love people—all kinds—their idiosyncrasies and all.

4. Have empathy for your participants; if you were in their shoes, you might also be rolling your eyes at the thought of a facilitated retreat.

5. Enjoy creating customized plans that inform, engage, and inspire teams to reach their goals.

6. Be able to think on your feet (literally) when your plans need to shift.

7. Know, as the driver of the bus, you must have the discipline to stay on track when you need to negotiate bumps, detours, storms, and complaining passengers to get your group to its destination.

8. Display confidence in yourself and your plan so your participants have the confidence to follow your lead.

9. Learn from every experience—what did and did not work—to continue to perfect your skills.

10. Get a real rush out of a well-planned day in which participants leave jazzed, enthusiastic, and prepared to move forward.

It takes work and thoughtful preparation—but there is a sense of achievement and joy in facilitating groups to help them clarify and solve their challenges, so they walk away feeling that THEY accomplished something important.

Our joy as facilitators is in knowing that we had a big part in making it happen—and that it probably would not have been as successful without our design preparation and our navigation throughout the day.

It's about making a difference for teams and companies—and in that comes satisfaction for a job well done.

Happy Facilitating!

ABOUT THE
AUTHOR

ABOUT THE AUTHOR

Mary Tomlinson

Mary Tomlinson has been facilitating meetings for nearly forty years (yes, she started VERY young!). Her passion for the subject came from years in corporate America enduring painfully long, unproductive meetings. She was convinced that there had to be a better way to engage individuals and their collective energy to solve problems.

Since 2001, Mary Tomlinson has been President of On-Purpose Partners, LLC, a facilitation, consulting, and coaching firm—where she specializes in the design and facilitation of planning retreats and workshops, personal/executive coaching, brand development, and customer service consulting.

Prior to starting her own business, Mary spent 18 years at the Walt Disney Company in several executive roles:

- Brand Director developing positioning strategy for Walt Disney World resorts and theme parks
- Business Director of Disney's internal advertising agency managing 5,000 projects with a $130 million budget
- Director of the former Disney Institute, a 585-room resort hotel and learning center with 800 employees, 100 training programs, and a $65 million budget

www.marytomlinson.com

MARY HAS BEEN DESCRIBED AS FOLLOWS

"Mary T's core is one of an optimistic connector—bringing energy, caring, broad awareness, humor, and sensitivity to helping people feel a sense of belonging and partnering with organizations to find solutions to issues."

HER FACILITATION CLIENTS HAVE SAID

"I want to thank you for the terrific and professional job facilitating our Executive Retreat and look forward to working with you many more times. Your knowledge, energy, and organization couldn't have been better. We all came away from the session much more aligned due to your leadership in facilitation."

General Manager

Walt Disney World Swan and Dolphin Resort

"I have been chairing a Faculty Compensation Taskforce for two years now, and with Mary's help, we are now finally ready to move towards closure on this issue. Mary did a fabulous job facilitating a very difficult topic. This was the most productive meeting we have had on this issue to date and we could not have done it without her. I have received comments from people saying that this was the best-run session they have ever attended at Valencia Community College."

Faculty Compensation Taskforce

Valencia College

"It was truly delightful to have Mary Tomlinson as our facilitator for the College Relations Advisory Board Meeting. Her uncanny knack to organize the meeting and drive our team to action was remarkable. Mary takes time to understand the uniqueness of each client. We couldn't be more pleased. She is truly an inspiration and has been significant in moving us in the right direction."

Director of College Relations

@ ARAMARK

NOTES

34693967R00060

Made in the USA
Middletown, DE
01 September 2016